DC SUPER HEROES
ANIMAL JOKES

BY MICHAEL DAHL
& DONALD LEMKE

STONE ARCH BOOKS
a capstone imprint

Published by Capstone Young Readers in 2018
A Capstone Imprint
1710 Roe Crest Drive
North Mankato, Minnesota 56003
www.capstonepub.com

STAR39967

Cataloging-in-Publication Data is available on the
Library of Congress website.

ISBN: 978-1-4965-5762-9 (library hardcover)
ISBN: 978-1-4965-5766-7 (eBook)

Summary: Why won't Wonder Woman's worst enemy fight fair?
Because she's a Cheetah! With dozens of ANIMAL jokes featuring
Batman, Superman, and Wonder Woman, readers will go wild
for this official DC Comics joke book!

Designer: Brann Garvey

Printed in China.
010734S18

HA!
HA!
HA!

DC SUPER HEROES
ANIMAL
JOKES

HA!
HA!
HA!

HA!
HA!
HA!

HA!
HA!
HA!

Why does Supergirl's cat, Streaky, keep running in circles?

Do you know how hard it is to run in squares?

Why did Wonder Woman's pet, Jumpa, go to the hospital?

She needed a hop-eration!

How did the octopus make Aquaman laugh?

With ten-tickles!

Why did Bumblebee have sticky hair?

Because she uses a honey-comb!

How did Krypto get away
from Lex Luthor?
He made his S-cape.

Why did Batman
arrest the sheep?
**It made
an illegal
ewe-turn!**

Did you hear the joke about the skunk
trapped in the Batmobile?
Never mind. It stinks!

What did Robin say when Catwoman
escaped from Arkham Asylum?
"It's a cat-astrophe!"

What did Robin get
when he trained with
a pig karate master?
**Pork
chops!**

When is the Joker like a pony?

When he's a little hoarse!

Who's the green super hero bovine
who comes from another planet?
The Martian Moo-hunter!

What do you call a
Bizarro flamingo?
A flamin-stop.

What do you call a Bizarro buffalo?
A buffa-high.

What do you get when you cross Cyborg with a pig?
A Cy-boar!

What do Green Arrow and a herd of cattle have in common?
Bull's-eyes.

Why did Killer Croc go to jail?
Because he's a crook-odile!

Which are the brightest pets
in Aquaman's kingdom?
The rays.

Do they serve crabs at
Aquaman's new restaurant?
They serve everybody. Have a seat!

What did Aquaman do when
he saw the blue whale?
Tried to cheer it up!

Where does Comet the
Super-Horse live?
In a neigh-borhood!

Why did Jumpa look so sad?
She was a little un-hoppy.

When does Comet the Super-Horse talk?
Whinny wants to!

Why can't Cheetah hide from Wonder Woman?
Because she's always spotted.

What happened when Cheetah stood behind Jumpa?
She got a real kick out of it!

Why doesn't Wonder Woman's
worst enemy fight fair?
**Because she's
a Cheetah!**

What do Cheetah and
The Flash have in common?
**They both like
fast food!**

What is Catwoman's favorite color?
Purr-ple.

Where is Catwoman's favorite
place to vacation?
Purrrr-u.

What happened when
a lion ate the Joker?
He felt funny!

Where should Streaky go if
he loses his tail?
A re-tail store.

What happened when Ace the
Bat-Hound swallowed a watch?
**He got a lot
of ticks!**

Why is Streaky the Super-Cat
a good crime fighter?
He can smell a rat.

DID YOU KNOW KRYPTO LIKES TO SMELL FLOWERS?

He's a bud hound!

What's Krypto's favorite dessert?
Pup-cakes!

Batman: "Where do fleas go in winter?"
Ace the Bat-Hound: "Search me!"

How is Ace the Bat-Hound
like a smartphone?
They both have collar I.D.!

Why doesn't Superman let Krypto
ever use his DVD player?
Because he always hits paws.

Where do Krypto, Ace the Bat-Hound,
and Streaky like to vacation?

The city of
Pet-ropolis!

What do you call a baby kanga that
always stays indoors?

A pouch potato.

How did Batman stop Ace the Bat-Hound from barking inside the Batcave?

He put him outside.

Why does Batman bring his pet when he chases after his enemy?

Because Ace always beats a Joker.

When does Batman take Ace for a walk?

When it's time to do his duty!

What is Beppo the Super-Monkey's favorite snack?

Chocolate chimp cookies!

How does Batman stay so clean?
**He takes a lot
of bats!**

What did Comet the Super-Horse
say when he tripped?
**I fell down, and
I can't giddy-up!**

What's Hawkwoman's
favorite dessert?
Magpie!

Where did Superman find
the missing lion?
On Mane Street!

Why can birds see Wonder Woman's Invisible Jet?

Because it's in di-skies!

Why did Hawkman and Hawkwoman
fly south for the winter?

**Because it was
too far to walk.**

What did Hawkwoman say
when she was cold?

Brrrrrrrrrd!

Why couldn't the Penguin pay
for dinner at the restaurant?

**His bill was
too big!**

Why didn't the octopus join
the Justice League?

**He was more suited
for the arm-y.**

What do you get when you cross
a waterfowl with Batman?
Goose Wayne!

What did Robin say when he saw
a low-flying bird?
"Duck!"

Which of Penguin's dirty birds
liked stealing things?
The robber ducky.

How many skunks could
fit in the Batmobile?
Quite a phew!

Why is Robin always so happy?
Because he's not a blue bird.

What do you get when you
cross Superman's girlfriend with
a bird that has long legs?
Lois Crane!

How does Shazam's Super-Pet,
Hoppy, go on vacation?
By Hare-plane.

How did the Penguin fly
south for the winter?
In his private jet.

Who's the green super hero duck
that comes from another planet?
Marshy Manhunter!

Why didn't the police
believe Cheetah?

They thought
she was a lion!

WHY WAS THE PENGUIN THROWN OFF THE BASEBALL TEAM?

He could only hit fowl balls!

Why are porcupines Green Arrow's
favorite animals?

**Because they have
a lot of quills.**

Why did the lemur have
rings on its tail?

**It hoped to become
a Green Lantern!**

Where did the two Amazon
rodents come from?
Pair-O-Mice Island!

What kind of book does Wonder
Woman's kanga like to read?
One with a hoppy
ending!

Why did Wonder Woman take her kanga to the hospital?

She needed a hop-eration.

What happened when Superman skipped college and flew to the Sun?

He got a million degrees!

How does Green Lantern spend his time in art class?

Color-ring.

When Solomon Grundy was young there were only 25 letters in the alphabet.

Nobody new why.

Why is Ace the Bat-Hound always on time?

He's a great watch dog!

What is Titano's favorite month?
Ape-ril!

Why did Titano climb up the side of the building?
The elevator was broken!

Why does Beppo the Super-Monkey
like bananas so much?

They have appeal.

How does a super hero
elephant ride to work?

In a trunk!

What sickness does Comet the
Super-Horse hate the most?

Hay fever.

What does Supergirl give Comet
to make him feel better?

Cough stirrup!

How did Superman stop the runaway elephant from charging?
He took away its credit card.

WHAT DO YOU CALL KILLER CROC IN A VEST?

An investigator.

BIZARRO'S OPPOSITE JOKES!

What do you get when you cross
Bizarro with a chameleon?
A chamele-off!

What do you get when you cross
Bizarro with a bison?
A bi-daughter.

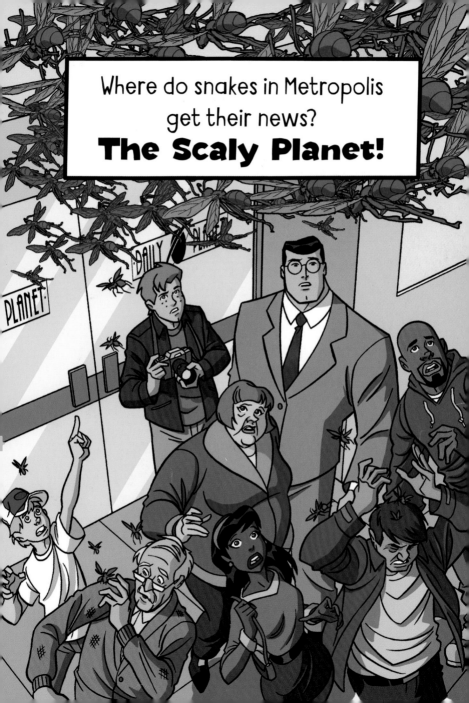

What do get when you cross
Superman's worst enemy with
a dinosaur?

Rex Luthor!

Why did Commissioner Gordon need help arresting an octopus?
Because it was heavily armed.

Why did Aqualad bring
fish to the party?

**They taste good
with chips!**

What do you get when you cross a
shrimp with Green Lantern?

Prawn Stewart!

What did Krypto the Super-Dog say when he sat on sandpaper?
Ruff!

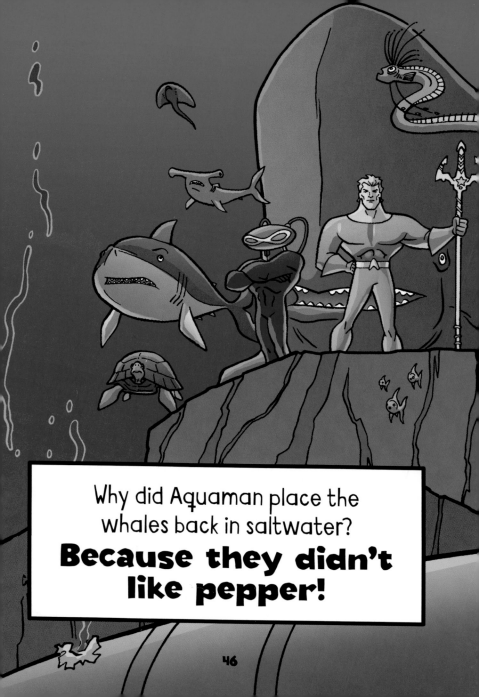

Why did Aquaman place the whales back in saltwater?

Because they didn't like pepper!

Why did Aquaman need help
capturing an octopus?

**Because the octopus
was well-armed.**

Why did Aquaman's seahorse,
Storm, cross the ocean?

**To get to the
other tide!**

Why does Aquaman command
seagulls to fly over the sea?

**If they flew over
the bay, they'd be
called bagels!**

What do you get when you cross a great white with Superman?

Shark Kent!

Why did Aqualad need an umbrella under water?

Because it was raining catfish and dogfish!

How do Aquaman and Mera communicate under the sea?

With shell-phones!

Why did Hawkman make a valentine for Hawkgirl in art class?

They were tweet-hearts!

Why did Cyborg buy a great white shark?

Because he wanted more bytes.

Which sea creature is almost as speedy as The Flash? **The Fastest Manta-live!**

Which of Aquaman's ocean creatures cries the most?

The humpback wail!

Why did Aquaman order the elephants off the beach?

Their trunks were too big!

What do you get when you cross an oyster with a Kryptonian?

Super-pearl!

Where does Aquaman
listen to music?
At the orca-stra!

What is Aquaman's favorite
country to visit?
Fin-land!

Why are Aquaman's underwater
friends so smart?
Because fish live
in schools.

What's invisible and smells
like bananas?
Titano burps!

What do you get when Mr. Freeze forgets
to put on his pants?

A polar bare!

What kind of pet does
Mr. Freeze have?

Coldfish.

How did the Penguin know
it was raining cats and dogs?
**He stepped in
a poodle!**

Where does the Penguin
keep his money?
**In a snow
bank!**

What does the Penguin
wear on his head?
An ice cap.

Why don't alligators like to eat the Joker?

He tastes funny!

What's the difference between a fly and Superman?

Superman can fly, but a fly can't Superman!

Where did the Super-Turtle get a new shell?
The hard-wear store!

HOW TO TELL JOKES!

1. KNOW the joke.

Make sure you remember the whole joke before you tell it. This sounds like a no-brainer, but most of us have known someone who says, "Oh, this is so funny . . ." Then, when they tell the joke, they can't remember the end. And that's the whole point of a joke — its punch line.

2. SPEAK CLEARLY.

Don't mumble; don't speak too fast or too slow. Just speak like you normally do. You don't have to use a different voice or accent or sound like someone else.

3. LOOK at your audience.

Good eye contact with your listeners will grab their attention.

4. DON'T WORRY about gestures or how to stand or sit when you tell your joke. Remember, telling a joke is basically talking.

5. DON'T LAUGH at your own joke.

Yeah, yeah, I know some comedians break up while they're acting in a sketch or telling a story, but the best rule to follow is not to laugh. If you start to laugh, you might lose the rhythm of your joke or keep yourself from telling the joke clearly. Let your audience laugh. That's their job. Your job is to be the funny one.

6. THE PUNCH LINE is the most important part of the joke.

It's the climax, the payoff, the main event. A good joke can sound even better if you pause for just a second or two before you deliver the punch line. That tiny pause will make your audience mentally sit up and hold their breath, eager to hear what's coming next.

7. The SETUP is the second most important part of a joke.

That's basically everything you say before you get to the punch line. And that's why you need to be as clear as you can (see 2) so that when you finally reach the punch line, it makes sense!

8. YOU CAN GET FUNNIER.

It's easy. Watch other comedians. Listen to other people tell a joke or story. Check out a good comedy show or film. You can pick up some skills simply by seeing how others get their comedy across. You will absorb it! And soon it will come naturally.

9. Last, but not least, telling a joke is all about TIMING.

That means not only getting the biggest impact for your joke, waiting for the right time, giving that extra pause before the punch line — but it also means knowing when NOT to tell a joke. When you're among friends, you can tell when they'd like to hear something funny. But in an unfamiliar setting, get a "sense of the room" first. Are people having a good time? Or is it a more serious event? A joke has the most funny power when it's told in the right setting.

MICHAEL DAHL

Michael Dahl is the prolific author of the bestselling *Goodnight, Baseball* picture book and more than 200 other books for children and young adults. He has won the AEP Distinguished Achievement Award three times for his nonfiction, a Teacher's Choice award from *Learning* magazine, and a Seal of Excellence from the Creative Child Awards. And he has won awards for his board books for the earliest learners, *Duck Goes Potty* and *Bear Says "Thank You!"* Dahl has written and edited numerous graphic novels for younger readers, authored the Library of Doom adventure series, the Dragonblood books, Trollhunters, and the Hocus Pocus Hotel mystery/comedy series. Dahl has spoken at schools, libraries, and conferences across the US and the UK, including ALA, AASL, IRA, and Renaissance Learning. He currently lives in Minneapolis, Minnesota, in a haunted house.

DONALD LEMKE

Donald Lemke works as a children's book editor. He has written dozens of all-age comics and children's books for Capstone, HarperCollins, Running Press, and more. Donald lives in St. Paul, Minnesota, with his brilliant wife, Amy, two toddling toddlers, and a not-so-golden retriever named Paulie.

JOKE DICTIONARY!

bit (BIT)—a section of a comedy routine

comedian (kuh-MEE-dee-uhn)—an entertainer who makes people laugh

headliner (HED-lye-ner)—the last comedian to perform in a show

improvisation (im-PRAH-vuh-ZAY-shuhn)—a performance that hasn't been planned; "improv" for short

lineup (LINE-uhp)—a list of people who are going to perform in a show

one-liner (WUHN-lye-ner)—a short joke or funny remark

open mike (OH-puhn MIKE)—an event at which anyone can use the microphone to perform for the audience

punch line (PUHNCH line)—the words at the end of a joke that make it funny or surprising

shtick (SHTIK)—a repetitive, comic performance or routine

segue (SEG-way)—a sentence or phrase that leads from one joke or routine to another

stand-up (STAND-uhp)—the type of comedy performed while standing alone on stage

timing (TIME-ing)—the use of rhythm and tempo to make a joke funnier

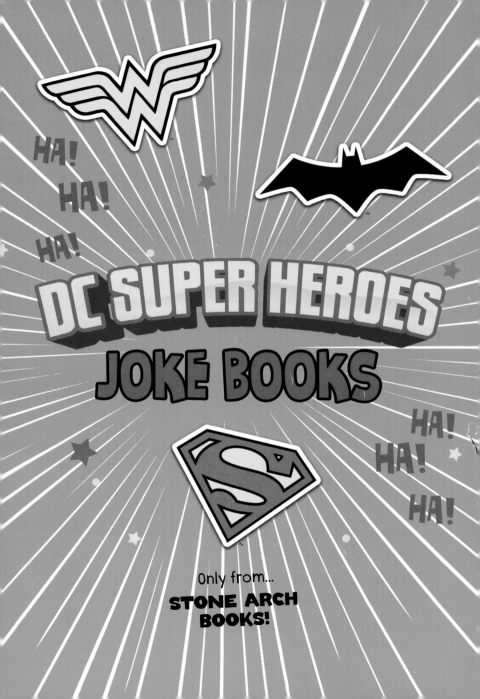

HA!

HA!

HA!

DC SUPER HEROES

JOKE BOOKS

HA!

HA!

HA!

Only from...

**STONE ARCH
BOOKS!**

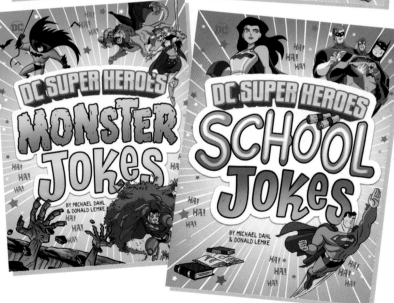